FERRARI *PHOTO GALLERY*

FERRARI
PHOTO GALLERY

by
Ippolito Alfieri

AUTOMOBILIA

Publisher
Bruno Alfieri

Editors
Valentina Lovetti
Saveria Tolomeo

Art Director
Fayçal Zaouali

Translated from Italian by
Elizabeth J. Poore

CL 41-0389-0   ISBN 88-7960-035-4
Printed and bound in Italy
by Grafiche Editoriali Padane, Cremona, June, 1998.
All rights are reserved
© Copyright 1998 by Automobilia
Società per la Storia e l'Immagine dell'Automobile
Milan, via Alberto Mario 16
Tel. (02) 48021428 – 48021481 – 48021671
Fax (02) 48194968

Contents

Ferrari's beginnings.

When Enzo Ferrari founded the company Auto Avio Costruzioni on the premises of the ex Scuderia Ferrari in Modena in 1939, he was 41 years old, and he had a strong desire to make a come-back. He had twenty years of experience under his belt gained at De Vecchi and CMN (Costruzioni Meccaniche Nazionali) of Milan as a driver – and a good driver too – although he never raced in a Grand Prix. He was registered by Alfa Romeo for the 1924 Lyons Grand Prix, but he never turned up at the start. Ferrari had developed his character and his professional experience in Alfa Romeo, the company that was his real school of life and his passion for that long period of time.

In December 1930 he had founded the Scuderia Ferrari in Modena, in via Trento e Trieste, after Alfa Romeo had decided to give up its racing team because of the depression. Ferrari created a stable of his own, with a prancing horse as the trademark, and continued to race the cars built by the Portello company (Alfa Romeo). He was also involved in their design with excellent results.

The Scuderia Ferrari lasted from 1930 to 1939, and at the same time Ferrari became the Alfa Romeo dealer for Emilia Romagna and the Marches. He had already fully understood the importance of competitions for the reputation of the automotive industry, as moreover Fiat, Lancia, Bugatti and all the other important makers had.

When he left Alfa Romeo dramatically in 1939 as a result of disagreement with the new Managing Director Ricart, Ferrari was too young and clever to spend his time making machine tools (grinders) for his workshop, and so in 1940 he was working on a roadster – the 815 – for the Mille Miglia. Bearing the trademark Auto Avio Costruzioni (Ferrari could not yet use his own name according to the terms of the contract), the car was an 8-cylinder 1.5 litre roadster, with an elegant body crafted by Touring of Milan, Alfa Romeo's bodymaker.

The dramatic upheaval of the Second World War and the bombings forced Ferrari to transfer to Maranello, a pretty town on the road to Abetone, where his father had left him some

land, and there he kept going, building machine tools under German licence. They were made so well that they worked better – it was said – than the original ones produced in Germany, showing Ferrari's passion for mechanics and the skill of the Modenese workers.

As is well known, as soon as the war was finished, Ferrari called Gioachino Colombo to Modena in August 1945; he was unemployed because of the destruction of the Alfa Romeo factories, and he was asked to design an exceptional engine: a V-12.

In addition to his passion for fine mechanics, Ferrari had always shown great discernment in his choice of designers, starting from Vittorio Jano, who he had stolen from Fiat for Alfa Romeo. Colombo was an excellent designer and when Ferrari asked him for a 12-cylinder (which he had already thought of before the meeting, since he knew the Commendatore's *preference for this type of engine, admired as a soldier under the Packard bonnets of the American officers serving in Italy), he didn't bat an eye. He went back to Milan and immediately designed the first*

plurifractionated Ferrari engine. It was destined for a car which was all engine with a very narrow cabin: the 125 S. The car, which was also made in a Grand Prix version, was not particularly beautiful, but its engine was a treasure and already on May 25, 1947, driven by Franco Cortese, it beat all competitors at the Rome Grand Prix, raced on the amazing Fori Romani circuit, beside the Terme di Caracalla. It was the first of hundreds of other victories all over the world for Ferrari.

Enzo Ferrari photographed during an interview with Griffith Borgeson, 1981.

*Brescia, April 28,1940.
A historic moment:
the Auto Avio
Costruzioni 815,
the first car made by
Enzo Ferrari, is about to
start on its début race,
the 1940 Mille Miglia.
At the wheel is Alberto
Ascari, future Formula 1
World Champion with
his cousin Giovanni
Minozzi at his side.
They had to withdraw
from the race about
halfway through
because of
mechanical problems.*

Towards success: the first racing cars.

When Enzo Ferrari first started his company, he did not have great economic resources but this did not discourage him, or frustrate his ambitions. The first cars were assembled in artisan fashion, by hand, using universal parts and recycling from one model to another as much as possible. Not even the spark plugs were thrown away, and it should be remembered that the Ferrari engines had at least a dozen and sometimes even twenty-four spark plugs.

Continuous improvement of models was the fundamental key to the first successes in competitions. And naturally the enthusiasm, and the desire to build something 'big'. At the end of the forties Ferrari could boast success in some of the most prestigious races like the Mille Miglia, the Targa Florio, and the Le Mans 24 Hours. These successes were a reason for pride, but not for losing one's head: Ferrari liked to maintain in fact that 'it is much easier to get to the top than to stay at the top'.

As part of this constant process of improvement, the Ferrari engines increased progressively in size in search of new power, and the mechanics was increasingly refined. After the 125, came the 166, the 195 and the 212, the models designed for road or endurance races. For the Grand Prix races of Formula 1 and 2 there were the 125, the 159, the 166, the 275, the 340 and the 375. Driving a 375 F1, the Argentinian driver Froilan Gonzalez brought Ferrari its first victory in a race that was valid for the Formula 1 World Championship, the 1951 British Grand Prix on the Silverstone circuit. It was a great day, almost a victory of David against Goliath: for the first time Ferrari succeeded in defeating the invincible Alfa Romeos. Enzo Ferrari then wrote in his memoirs that he cried with joy when victory was announced: 'revenge' against the red Alfa Romeo single-seater was complete, and Ferrari could finally look ahead and aim much higher.

July 14, 1951.
British Grand Prix,
Silverstone.
Perhaps the most
exciting day of all
for Enzo Ferrari.
The Argentinian driver
Froilan Gonzalez,
in the 375 F1, made
the first win for Ferrari
in a Grand Prix race
valid for the World
Championship, beating
their very strong rivals,
the Alfettas. For Ferrari
this success represented
a sort of revenge over
Alfa Romeo.

15

The 166 MM barchetta, with a body by Carrozzeria Touring, of Milan. The model shown is the one with which Luigi Chinetti and Selsdon won the 1949 Le Mans 24 Hours. The number '22' is still the race number which the American collector who owns the car carefully maintains.

Preceding page. June 24-25, 1950. Le Mans 24 Hours. The two 166 MM Ferraris driven by Rubirosa/Leygonie and Lucas/Selsdon are hard at work on the famous White House 'S' bend on the Sarthe circuit. On this occasion Lord Selsdon did not succeed in repeating the success of the previous year gained together with Chinetti at the wheel of a totally identical car. Overall Ferrari had nine wins in the most famous endurance race in the world.

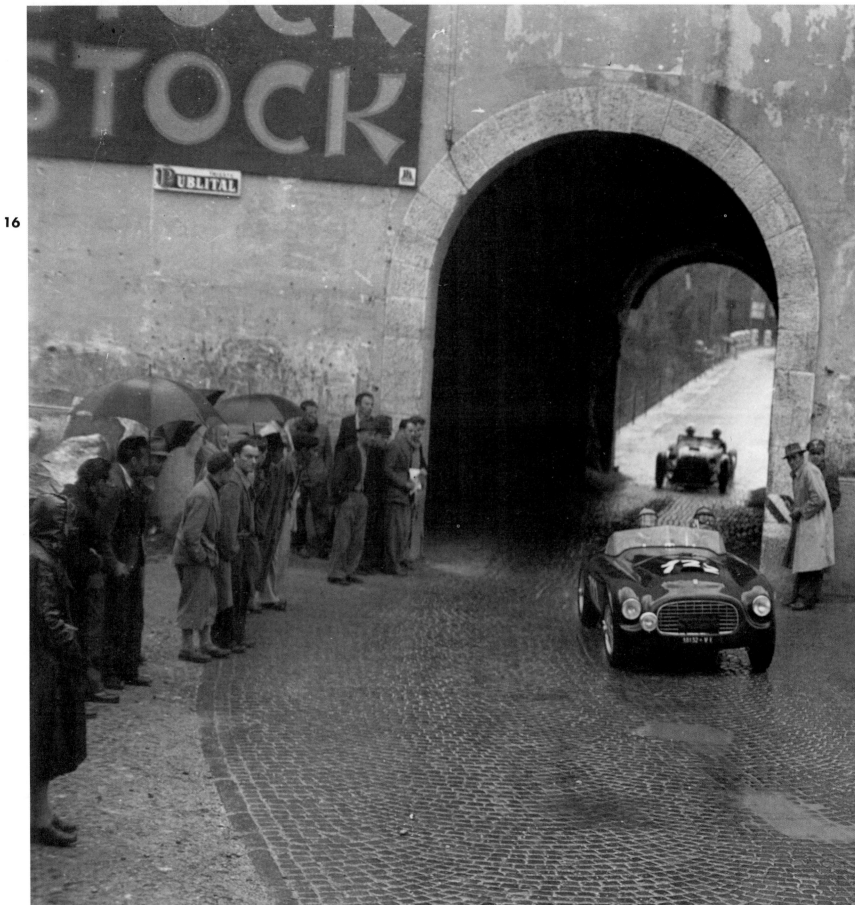

April 23, 1950.
Mille Miglia.
Vittorio Marzotto
and Paolo Fontana
on a Ferrari 166 MM
go through Peschiera.
The Marzotto family,
famous for production
of textiles, has its name
inextricably linked to
that of Ferrari, and
won many races with
Prancing Horse cars.
In the Mille Miglia of
that year there were
four members of the
Marzotto family
participating: Vittorio
who arrived ninth,
Umberto and Paolo
both on Ferrari
166 MMs that were
forced to withdraw,
and Giannino who
won at the wheel
of a Ferrari 195 S.

From racing to GTs.

The very first Ferraris were racing cars that were used in competitions by the company or alternatively by private drivers who bought them directly from the factory. Very soon however Ferrari realized that clients did not only want to race his cars, but they also wanted to drive them normally on normal roads. So he decided to satisfy this demand by 'taming' his racing cars. Thus the first touring cars came into being, or rather, given their performance, the first 'granturismo' cars.

But Ferrari's real flash of intuition was in another field. Refined mechanics and high performance alone in fact would not have been enough to transform Ferrari into the mythical carmaker that it has become today. Ferrari wanted his GTs to be beautiful as well as fast, and to achieve this he worked with the best Italian bodymakers of the time. He worked with Vignale, Touring, Bertone, Zagato, and Ghia, who all 'clothed' Ferraris' mechanical bodies. In fact Ferrari called them his 'tailors'.

Some of the bodies made for the mechanics of the 166 MM and Inter, the 195 Inter, the 212 Inter and Export are unforgettable masterpieces. Still today they are breathtaking for their elegance, their superb shapes, and their extreme attention to detail. Ferrari owes much of his success to these bodymakers, but he found the form he was really seeking only in one of them: Giovan Battista 'Pinin' Farina. Collaboration with the Turin bodymaker began in 1952 after a first meeting with Ferrari and 'Pinin' Farina which took place in a restaurant in Tortona. The two companies still collaborate.

It was from GTs sales that Ferrari managed to obtain the resources necessary to race. By winning races he built a solid reputation which enabled him to further increase sales of the GTs. In a short time Ferrari had become a full-blooded carmaker, specialized in the construction of racing cars and GTs.

At the end of the forties, after a number of years devoted exclusively to racing, Enzo Ferrari began to build touring cars. The model shown is one of the first: it is a 166 Inter with a 1949 Touring body.

The 1955 375 Plus
is one of the most
beautiful GTs ever made
by Ferrari. Pinin Farina's
ability to combine
elegant harmony and
aggressive traits is
absolutely amazing.

Ferrari: World Champion.

Winning one or two battles does not necessarily mean winning the war. The victories obtained from 1947 to 1952 were, metaphorically speaking, the battles which brought Ferrari into the limelight. But the definitive consecration of Ferrari came only with the world title.

The first in what was to be a long series of triumphs was won in 1952, thanks to the extraordinary qualities of the Ferrari 500 F2 and its driver Alberto Ascari.

The Milanese driver repeated his exploit the following year. He was the last Italian to win the F1 title, but in the fifties another two Ferrari drivers succeeded in winning the Championship: the Argentinian Juan Manuel Fangio in 1956 and the Englishman Mike Hawthorn in 1958.

But the public of the time was more interested in the Sports category than in Formula 1, unlike today. The drivers also raced in both categories.

In 1953 the FIA started the World Manufacturers' Championship and Ferrari was the first carmaker to win it. And continued to win it every year until 1964, with only two exceptions: in 1954 Mercedes-Benz won, and in 1959 Aston Martin, although the FIA tried to break Ferrari's hold through constant and sometimes sudden changes in the regulations. Enzo Ferrari was very annoyed by this obstructionist attitude, and threatened a number of times to withdraw, but continued to win road and track races all over the world.

The mythical status of the Prancing Horse was built largely on the amazing wins by the 12-cylinder Ferrari Sports cars, but also the 4-cylinder and the 6-cylinder. The red Ferrari cars regularly won the Mille Miglia, and the Le Mans 24 Hours, but they also managed to win just as easily on the unsealed roads of the Carrera Panamericana Mexico, on the hundred and more curves of the demanding Nürburgring circuit, at home on the very fast Monza track, and even in the uphill races.

At the end of the fifties Ferrari could boast nine world titles in Formula 1 and Sports races. The lesser wins, at national and international level, were already so numerous that they could no longer easily be counted.

September 1953, Monza Autodrome. From the left, Luigi Villoresi, Alberto Ascari and Enzo Ferrari pose smiling for a souvenir photo. Ferrari had already won two world titles at this stage, with Alberto Ascari, World Champion in 1952 and in 1953. After Ascari no Italian ever succeeded again in becoming Formula 1 World Champion.

September 13, 1953. Italian Grand Prix, Monza. Ascari on a Ferrari ahead of Marimon on a Maserati, Farina on a Ferrari, and Fangio on a Maserati. Fangio won after a spectacular accident on the last lap. Ascari still won the world title, even although he had to withdraw; he had won 5 times in 9 races during the season.

April 26, 1953.
Mille Miglia. The
Marzotto/Crosara team
on a Ferrari 340 MM
at the Rome checkpoint.
They won the race
ahead of Fangio's
Alfa Romeo 3000 and
Bonetto's Lancia D20,
putting a large distance
between them and
their rivals. This was
Marzotto's second
victory in the Mille
Miglia, the most
prestigious road
race of the time.

Accidents are always
possible in races.
In its racing career
Ferrari's name has been
associated with many
wins and also with
some accidents.
Some were spectacular
like this one involving
Umberto Marzotto in
the 1950 Mille Miglia.

Opposite page.
Eugenio Castellotti
on a Ferrari 290 MM,
winner of the 1956
Mille Miglia.

32 *Piero Taruffi on a Ferrari 315 S crosses the finishing line and wins the 1957 Mille Miglia. The race was devastated by a tragic accident where De Portago left the road on his Ferrari at 300 km/h, killing himself, his co-driver Nelson and eleven spectators. After the accident which happened near Mantova, the Mille Miglia was abolished.*

This page. The English driver Peter Collins, also on a Ferrari 315 S at the Rome checkpoint. In the lead for over half of the race, Collins withdrew when a tyre burst.

Following pages. Olivier Gendebien and Paul Frère, winners of the 1960 Le Mans 24 Hours, in a Ferrari 250 Testa Rossa.

Kings, millionaires and stars driving Ferraris.

With the very first GTs, Ferrari managed to seduce those who particularly loved the mechanics and performance of his cars. But from the second half of the fifties onwards, Ferrari opened up towards a wealthier international clientèle, including kings, magnates, and stars.

The winning card for success was now primarily beauty. A type of beauty that bewitched people like King Leopold of Belgium, Prince Bernard of Holland, the Shah of Persia, the King of Morocco, Gianni Agnelli, Anna Magnani, Roberto Rossellini, Catherine Deneuve, Paul Newman, and Frank Sinatra. Famous personalities who were bewitched by the Prancing Horse cars, and couldn't resist them.

Ferrari was aware of how much people liked his cars and he often allowed himself the pleasure of 'torturing' his clients: once a car had been ordered and customized according to the taste of the purchaser, a number of months could pass before it was delivered. As soon as it was ready, the client was summoned to Maranello where he or she was often subjected to an exhausting long wait in the waiting room. Only the 'favourite' clients were allowed to have the car delivered directly.

His character aside, Ferrari was aware of how important the proceeds from sales were and, in his heart, he had a deep form of respect for his clients. 'To sell we have to win races, but to win races we have to sell', he would say.

Very soon Ferrari's biggest market was the United States. Some models were given names clearly inspired by this: 342 America, 400 Superamerica, 250 GT California. This phenomenon seems very curious if we remember the strict speed limits on American roads. But Ferraris were venerated by Americans for their beauty rather than their performance. An American client who was particularly in love with his car, put it in the middle of his living room and never drove it. Ferraris began to be cult objects outside Italy long before they were in Italy.

*1964. Pininfarina
plants, Grugliasco.
From left: Pinin Farina,
Enzo Ferrari, Pinin's
son Sergio, and Prince
Bernard of Holland.
The commercial
success of the Ferrari
GTs depended in large
part also on the VIPs
who became devoted
clients of Ferrari
from the fifties.*

*Following pages.
One of the most
beautiful Ferraris ever
made was without doubt
the 250 GT California
roadster of which
only slightly more
than a hundred were
built between the
end of the fifties
and the early sixties.*

The rear engine revolution.

'Oxen have always pulled carts, they never push them'. This was Enzo Ferrari's answer to his technicians who tried to convince him to abandon the front engine position of his racing cars, and to change to the rear, following the example of the English carmakers. In reality, without needing to imitate his competitors, Enzo Ferrari had already understood himself that the future was for rear-engined cars, but he was waiting for the right moment to put what was to be the first 'technical revolution' to take place at Maranello into effect.

After a few test races in Formula 1 in 1960, from 1961 the engine moved behind the driver, both in the single-seater and the Sports vehicles. Already in the first year the rear engine won the first in a whole series of world titles: success went to the American Phil Hill who defeated his team mates Von Trips and Ginther. At the same time, in 1961, Ferrari won the World Manufacturers' title with the Sports cars.

For reasons of bulk the engine was no longer a 12-cylinder, but a 6-cylinder, whose design had also been worked on by Enzo Ferrari's son, Dino, who tragically died very young of a terrible disease.

In 1964 Ferrari won another Formula 1 title with John Surtees, who was already a world motorcycling champion, and the only driver to win both two and four wheel titles.

But front-engined racing cars were still popular. In the three years from 1962 to 1964 an extraordinary Ferrari, the 250 GTO, would bring Maranello three World Manufacturers' titles, completely wiping out its adversaries.

The rear engine revolution was completed definitively in 1967 when the engine was placed in the rear for the first time also on a series model, the Dino 206 GT, also with the 6-cylinder engine named after Ferrari's son. From this moment Ferrari would maintain the front engine position only on a few series models.

June 18, 1961.
Belgian Grand Prix,
Spa-Francorchamps.
This was one of the
most memorable days
in Ferrari's history.
At the finish four Ferraris
finished in the first four
places. Phil Hill was
ahead of Von Trips,
Ginther and Gendebien,
in that order. Hill won
the world title at the
end of the season.

*1970. The Monza
1000 Km. Giunti and
Vaccarella's 512 S
(no. 3), Parkes and
Muller's 512 S (no. 8),
and Amon and
Merzario's 512 S
(no. 1).*

*Opposite page.
1971. Le Mans
24 Hours. The Ecurie
Francorchamps 512 M,
with de Fierlant and
de Cadenet.
They withdrew at the
18th hour after a very
hard-fought race.*

*This page. 1964.
Maranello. Enzo Ferrari
in a particularly good
mood during one
of the traditional meals
at the end of the year.
First on the left is John
Surtees, new Formula 1
World Champion.*

*Opposite page.
September 6, 1970.
Italian Grand Prix
Monza. Clay
Regazzoni on a Ferrari
312 takes first place.
The race was
blackened by the
Austrian driver Rindt's
fatal accident in the test
sessions; he won the
world title posthumously.*

This page.
April 25, 1972.
The Monza 1000 Km.
Big celebration at
Ferrari after the
Ickx/Regazzoni victory.
Ferrari had 12 wins
for 12 races in 1972,
and won its last World
Manufacturers' title
before withdrawing
from the Sportscar
category.

Opposite page.
February 6,1972.
Daytona 6 Hours.
Regazzoni with Redman
came fourth in the race
which was dominated
by the other two
Ferraris driven by
Andretti/Ickx and
Peterson/Scheckter,
who took the first
two places.

*June 10, 1973.
Le Mans 24 hours.
The 312 PB no.16
of Arturo Merzario
and Carlos Pace
which finished second.
At the end of 1973
Ferrari abandoned
the Sportscar category
definitively.*

Opposite page.
February 5, 1967.
Daytona 24 Hours.
The historical arrival
of the Ferrari 330 P4s.
The no. 23 with
Amon/Bandini,
the race winners;
Parkes/Scarfiotti
in second place
with no. 24;

Guichet/Rodriguez
with no. 26 in third
place. The photo
is autographed by
the drivers.

May 21, 1972.
Targa Florio. The Ferrari
312 PB of the winners
Merzario/Munari.
The Sicilian race,
as can be seen, was
raced over a normal
road where large
numbers of spectators
watched lined up only
a few metres from
the racing cars.

The fastest car in the world.

The dream of speed is one that man has always had. Supersonic planes, high-speed trains, superfast boats. And cars? Ferrari of course!

Already back in the sixties Ferraris had gained their reputation as 'the fastest cars in the world' with their mighty 12-cylinder engines, 'bullets' that could go as fast as three hundred kilometres an hour. Performances which are, today no less than then, difficult for any other car, at the limit of the impossible.

For a Ferrari, though, speed is an objective fact, as can be seen from the road test reported in the most important magazines in the world. But it is at the same time also a very abstract concept, related to the shape of the body. A Ferrari looks fast even when it is at a standstill because its lines transmit a sense of dynamism.

A typical example was without doubt the extraordinary 365 GTB/4 'Daytona' made by Ferrari in 1968. A 4400 cc engine, with 6 carburettors, 350 hp for a maximum speed of over 280 km/h. Ferrari had Pininfarina make a coupé version and a roadster (the famous roadster of the television series 'Miami Vice'). The 'Daytona' was an exceptional car not only because of its mechanics, but also because of beauty, dynamism and aggressiveness. It was an extraordinary success, also from the commercial point of view.

And it was not just a one-off masterpiece out of all the cars produced by the Maranello company. In addition to the unforgettable 'Daytona', Ferrari made many cars at that time that were just as fast and just as beautiful, like the 275 GTB of 1966, the Dino 246 GT and GTS of 1970 with the small 6-cylinder engine, the 365 GTB/4 Berlinetta Boxer of 1973, the 8-cylinder 308 GTB and GTS of 1975.

Model after model, the idea of speed was increasingly associated with the shield of the Prancing Horse. Internationally, the word Ferrari is nowadays synonymous with the word speed.

A striking view of a Ferrari 365 GTS 'Daytona' in New York. America is one of the places where the Ferrari myth is strongest.

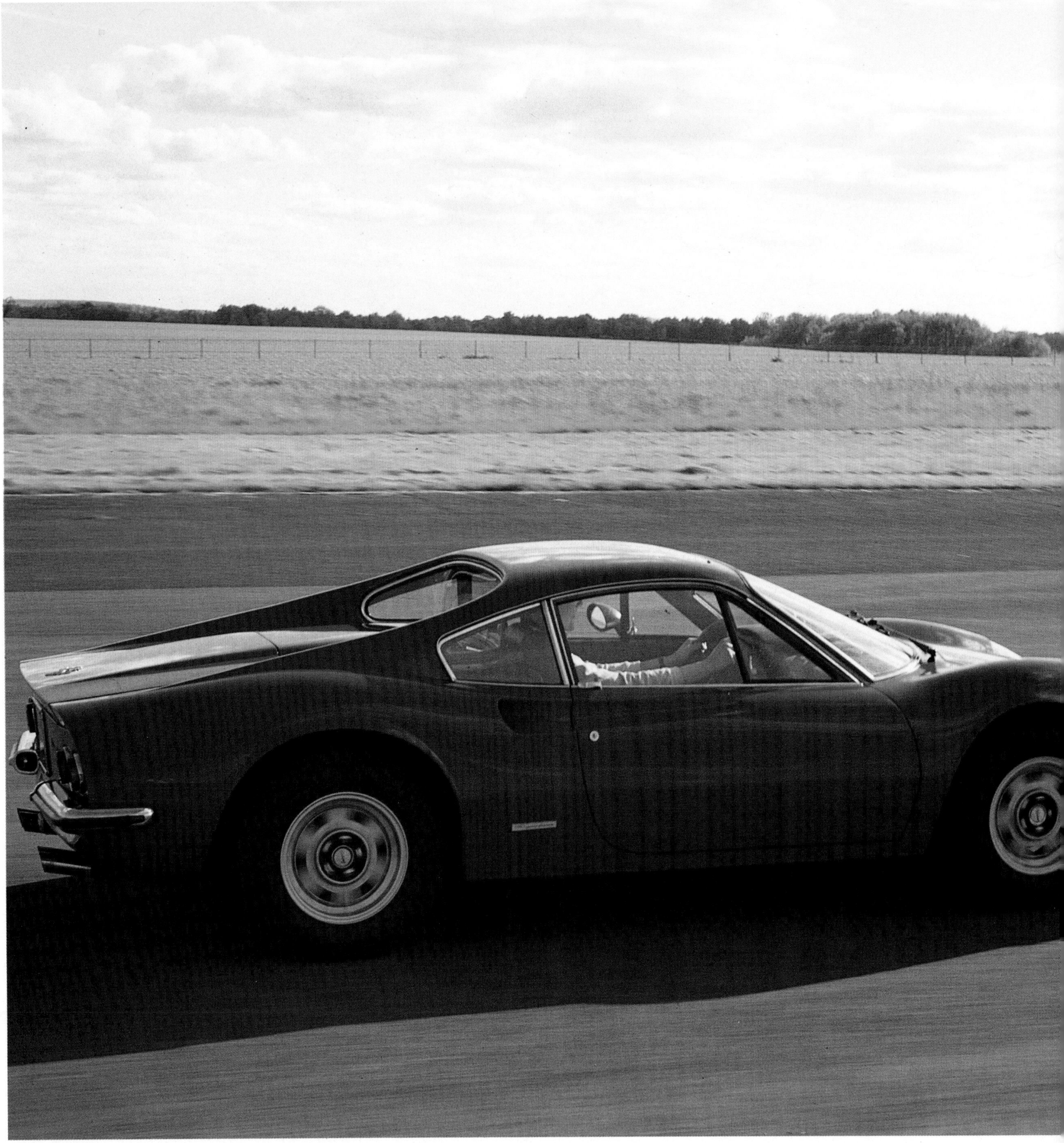

The Dino 246 GT of 1967 was the first road car with rear engine produced by the Maranello company.

Opposite page.
The 288 GTO
presented in 1984
is a supercar of which
270 units were built;
today it is one of the
most valuable Ferraris.

This page.
The 1987 F40 was
made to celebrate
Ferrari's first forty years
and is still stunning
because of its
aggressive lines. Over
1,000 units were built.
At the time it was the
fastest series car in the
world (324 km/h).

Following pages.
The Testarossa is
probably the best
known Ferrari of the
eighties and nineties.
A real star in terms
of image and
performance,
the Testarossa was
produced in three
different series up
to 1996.

Races: victories and problems.

62 *Michele Alboreto was official Formula 1 Ferrari driver from 1984 to 1988. Alboreto came close to winning the world title in 1985 and experienced at first hand both ups and downs in Ferrari, and both the joy and pain of the turbo era single-seaters.*

Ferrari raced in both Sports and Formula 1 categories only until the early seventies.

At a certain point Ferrari realized that for a company that built both frame and engine, commitment on two fronts required an effort that could no longer be sustained. In 1973 he therefore decided to continue only in Formula 1. The results proved the choice to be right. The amazing dynasty of the 312 T single-seaters brought Ferrari seven world titles between 1975 and 1979.

Behind these extraordinary years of success lay a team made up of exceptional designers, managers and drivers. Above all, there was a very young Team Manager, Luca di Montezemolo, an indefatigable designer, Mauro Forghieri, and a young Austrian driver, Niki Lauda, a real discovery. Enzo Ferrari had an extraordinary nose for new talents...

The relationship between two strong characters like Ferrari and Lauda was inevitably conflictual but was also very fruitful. Lauda won the world title in 1975 and in 1977 and Ferrari won the Constructors' title for three consecutive years, from 1975 to 1977. A year's wait and in 1979 another double victory: Jody Scheckter and Ferrari, World Champions.

After Lauda the rising star in car racing was also another previously totally unknown driver. The Canadian Gilles Villeneuve was to drive in some memorable races for Ferrari, before dying tragically during the Belgian Grand Prix trials.

In the eighties came the peak of the turbo engine era. Very quickly a power was achieved that was more appropriate for aeronautical than automobile engines, and the contribution of the driver became less and less important in comparison to the quality of the vehicle. These were difficult years for Ferrari, which nevertheless fought back bravely: two World Constructors' titles in 1982 and 1983 were an honourable booty in the light of the unequal challenge that the Prancing Horse had to face from enormous companies like Renault, Honda, and BMW.

May 11, 1975.
Monaco Grand Prix,
Monte Carlo. Niki
Lauda, winner of the
race, receiving the
trophy from Ranieri
and Grace of Monaco.

Luca di Montezemolo,
as a very young Team
Manager of Ferrari with
Niki Lauda (centre) and
Clay Regazzoni (right).
Under Montezemolo's
management Ferrari
won five world titles
(two Drivers' and three
Constructors') in the
three years from
1975 to 1977.

Maranello, 1980. Enzo Ferrari is affectionate with Gilles Villeneuve who was almost like a son for him.

Following pages. September 11, 1988, Italian Grand Prix, Monza. Less than a month after Enzo Ferrari's death, Berger (no. 28) and Alboreto (no. 27) win first and second place in the 'home' race.

Towards the year 2000.

On August 14, 1988 Enzo Ferrari died. Without the guiding light of its founder, Ferrari seemed to lose its way for a time: in the only category that it raced in, Formula 1, the results were poor, while production entered a somewhat wild phase with 4000 units produced a year, a number that the market could not support.

With the nomination of Luca di Montezemolo as Chairman of Ferrari in October 1991, a new chapter was opened in the history of the company. Montezemolo brought enthusiasm, new ideas, and reorganization to Ferrari: Ferrari took off towards the year 2000.

The first fruit of the new chapter was the 456 GT, presented in September 1992. A GT that, in addition to the usual exceptional performance, had qualities that up till that moment few had recognized in a Ferrari: habitability, versatility and comfort. All cars produced from now on expressed this more modern philosophy which attracted more clients to the trademark.

At the same time Ferrari discovered its role as a guiding light in research and development in carmaking: the F355, with 5 valves per cylinder and (from 1997) with gear change on the steering wheel, an innovation directly taken from racing cars; the F50, almost a Formula 1 car adapted to road use; the 550 Maranello, the fastest GT with front engine in the world, came into being. Competitors are way behind.

Luca di Montezemolo likes to say that Ferrari, as it moves towards the year 2000, is a healthy, dynamic, modern company. A company which produces thoroughbred cars including also the single-seaters for Formula 1. Nevertheless the merits of the new management are not limited to being forward-looking, but also to remembering the past. Ferraris today are authentic cult objects at international level: theme exhibitions, revivals, races for vintage models. The future, and also the past, seem to be in good hands.

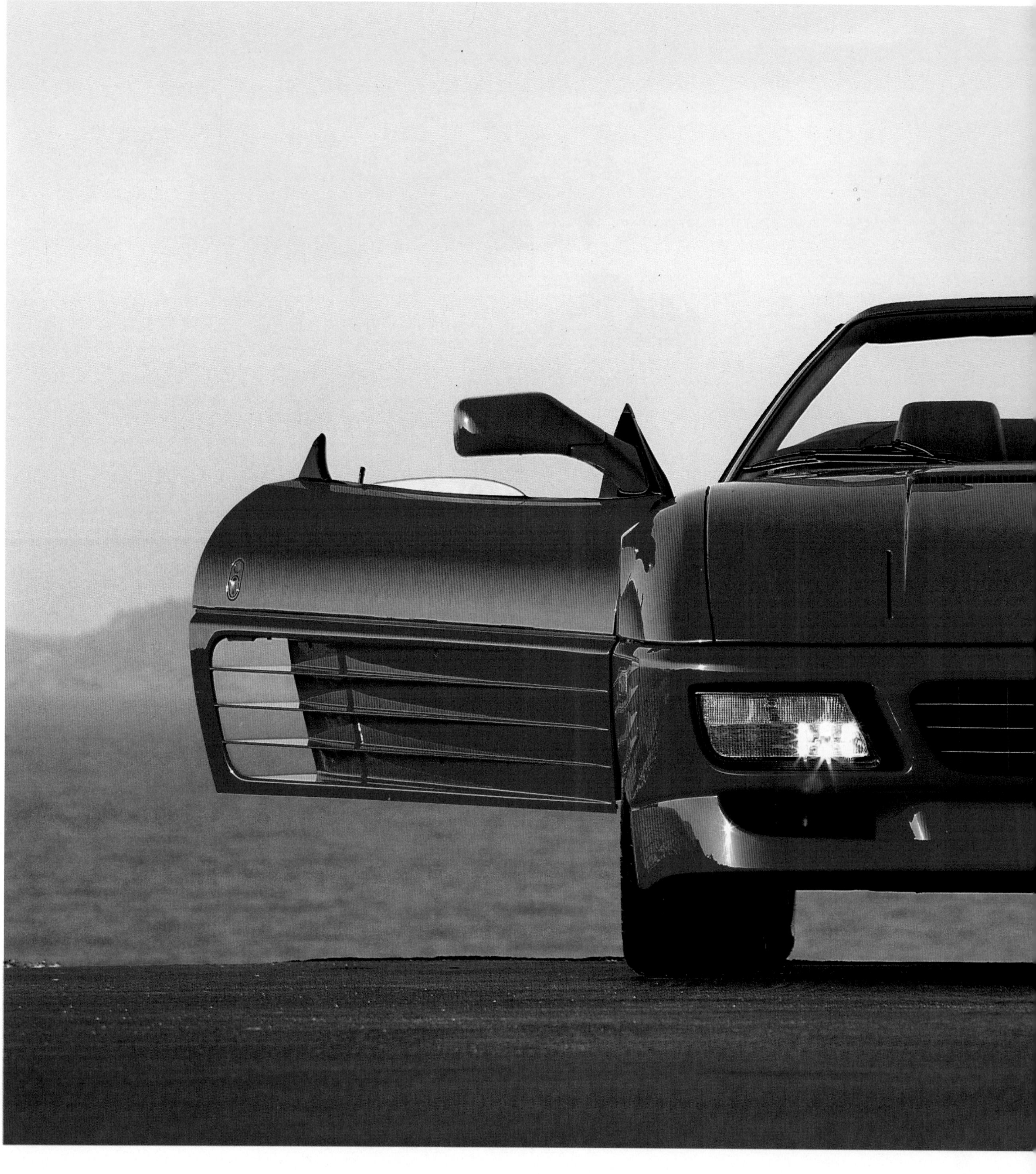

Everyone has asked themselves at least once how it is that Ferrari has become an authentic myth in our time. The answer perhaps is in this image which brings together in an exceptional way all the features of a Ferrari: beauty, aggressiveness, dynamism, elegance. The model shown is the 348 Spider of 1993.

For Ferrari enthusiasts, this is the 'small' Ferrari. The F355 in fact, with its 8-cylinder, 380 hp engine, is the least powerful Ferrari, but is still able to reach 295 km/h. There are three versions: Berlinetta, Spider and GTS. From 1997 it has also been available with automatic gear shift on the steering wheel, the same as the Formula 1 Ferraris of Schumacher (right) and Irvine.

74 *Ferrari safeguards its past very carefully with many shows, events and exhibitions. Opposite page, a rally of vintage Ferraris in Beverly Hills and, right, the inauguration of the Ferrari exhibition in 1993 at the Museum of Modern Art of New York.*

Opposite page. From 1993 Ferrari has made it possible for its clients to race in a single-mark trophy (Challenge) raced previously with the 348 and today with the F355.

This page. In 1997 a series Ferrari F355 did a 'World Tour' covering almost thirty thousand kilometres in numerous countries of all the continents.

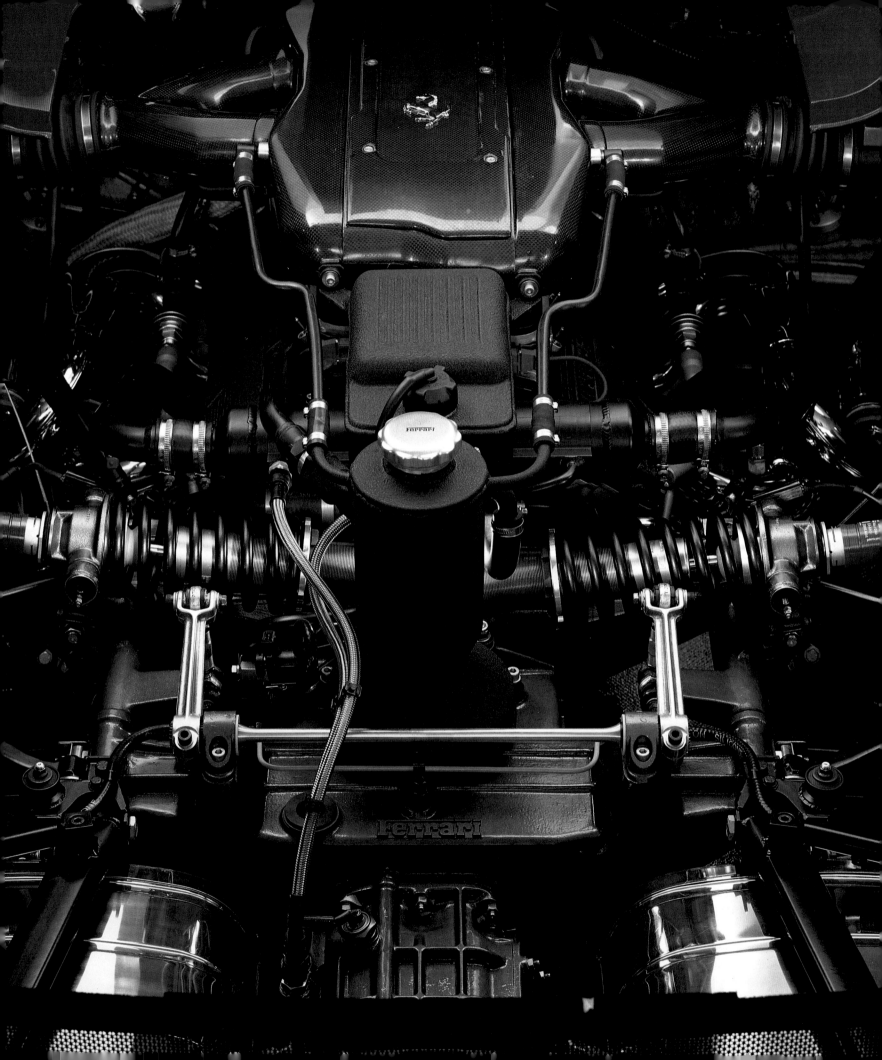

The F50 is Ferrari's most recent adventure in the fascinating world of supercars. The idea which inspired the F50 was to make a car, for the first time, with the technical characteristics of a F1 single-seater, but which could be used on the road. Only 349 units were built between 1995 and 1996. Its price at the time was 850 millions (Italian liras) and it could reach 325 km/h.

In 1996 Ferrari presented the 550 Maranello: with its return to the front engine, it is a revolution in the formula adopted for over twenty years in its more sporty GTs. This change was made to enable greater comfort and better habitability, without taking anything away from their excellent performance, a typical feature of Ferraris.

Ferrari, under the
management of Luca
di Montezemolo, is a
modern factory of sports
cars that does not forget
its roots. In May 1997,
for a whole week there
were celebrations for
the fiftieth anniversary
of the company's first
win in a race; they
took place in Rome,
(in the photo on
the opposite page)
Maranello and
Modena.

This page. From 1996
Shell sponsors the
homonymous Trophy,
which is made up of a
number of races, open
to racing Ferraris built
before 1973.

New scenarios for Formula 1.

Ferrari is the best-known and best-loved car stable in the world. Luca di Montezemolo maintains that one of the reasons for which the fans are so numerous outside Italy as well is because of the fact that Ferrari is the only team that flies its own flag instead of the national flag.

Formula 1 competition has led in recent years to an incredible acceleration in technology and the actors in the field are more numerous and aggressive than ever. But Ferrari, the only team to build both frames and engines itself, is fighting with great determination, and the red single-seaters continue to be both the symbol and the stars of the Grand Prix races.

In order to be able to face every new adversary, it was necessary to reorganize, and to renew work methodologies, and to find new economic resources. In a word, 'to change'.

Luca di Montezemolo, Chairman of Ferrari, called on Jean Todt to manage this ambitious project of transformation, and as well as maintenance of the spirit of Ferrari. Year after year, this process is now becoming reality. It has not been easy though. At the beginning of the nineties there were moments when the results were not in line with the name Ferrari. Drivers like Mansell, Prost, Berger, and Alesi have fought bravely, but with varying results.

Two years away from the fiftieth anniversary of the foundation of the Formula 1 World Championship, which Ferrari has always taken part in, the Maranello company can proudly claim to have all the right men in the right places. In the front line are the drivers, Michael Schumacher, who came to Ferrari in 1996 with two World Champion titles already under his belt, and Eddie Irvine. But behind the scenes a structure of at least four hundred people is working with dedication – the Sports Department – which enables the German champion to race and to win. And the contribution of the technical partners should not be forgotten, first of all Shell, which has shared many successes with Ferrari, right from the beginnings of racing in the fifties.

Racing, in this new scenario which is so competitive, is not easy. Winning even less so. So let's not forget this, every time a red single-seater crosses the finishing line first!

March 26, 1989. Brasilian Grand Prix, Interlagos. In the race which marked the return of normally-aspirated engines to Formula 1, Ferrari took first place with Nigel Mansell, the last driver personally chosen by Enzo Ferrari.

Following pages. Jean Alesi and his 'flaming' Ferrari 642 in the 1991 season.

Enzo Ferrari sought first and foremost courage in drivers. Those he loved most all had this quality. Jean Alesi, with Ferrari from 1991, did not know Ferrari personally, but his driving certainly embodied this quality.

Following pages. September 13, 1992. Italian Grand Prix, Monza. Alesi and Capelli insist on a Goodyear chicane during the race.

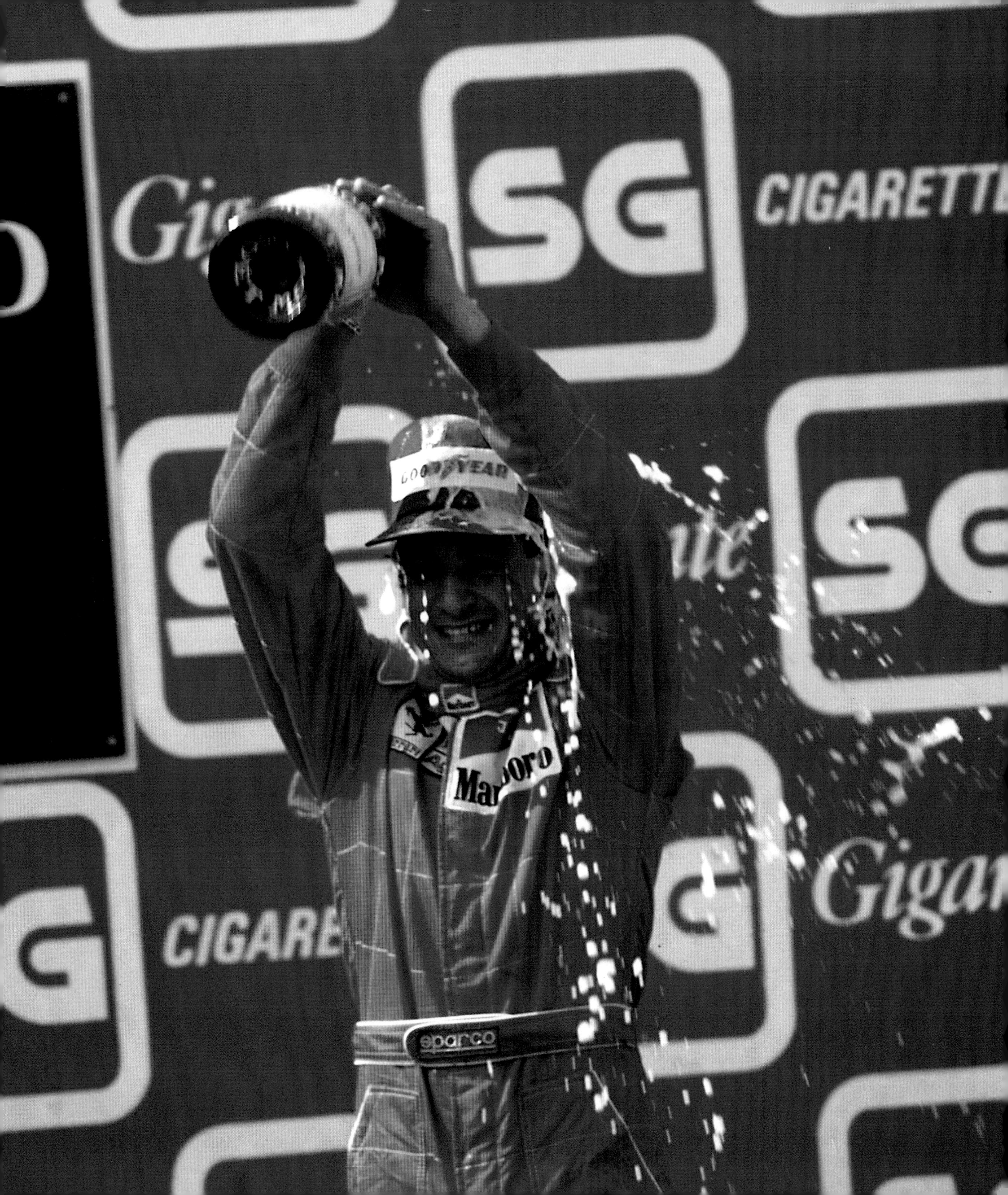
SG
GOODYEAR
sparco

94 *Transport costs are one of the heaviest items in the budget of a Formula 1 season. Air transportation to Japan can cost $ 750,000. In addition to the cars, there is a great deal of other equipment to be transported to Grand Prix races (pictures on this page).*

Following pages. Jean Alesi in the 1992 Monaco Grand Prix.

Jean Alesi in the 1993 British Grand Prix.

Gerhard Berger during the French Grand Prix trials in 1993.

Jean Alesi in a spectacular offgoing during the 1993 Hungarian Grand Prix.

Jean Alesi in the 1994 Brasilian Grand Prix.

Jean Alesi in the 1994 Belgian Grand Prix.

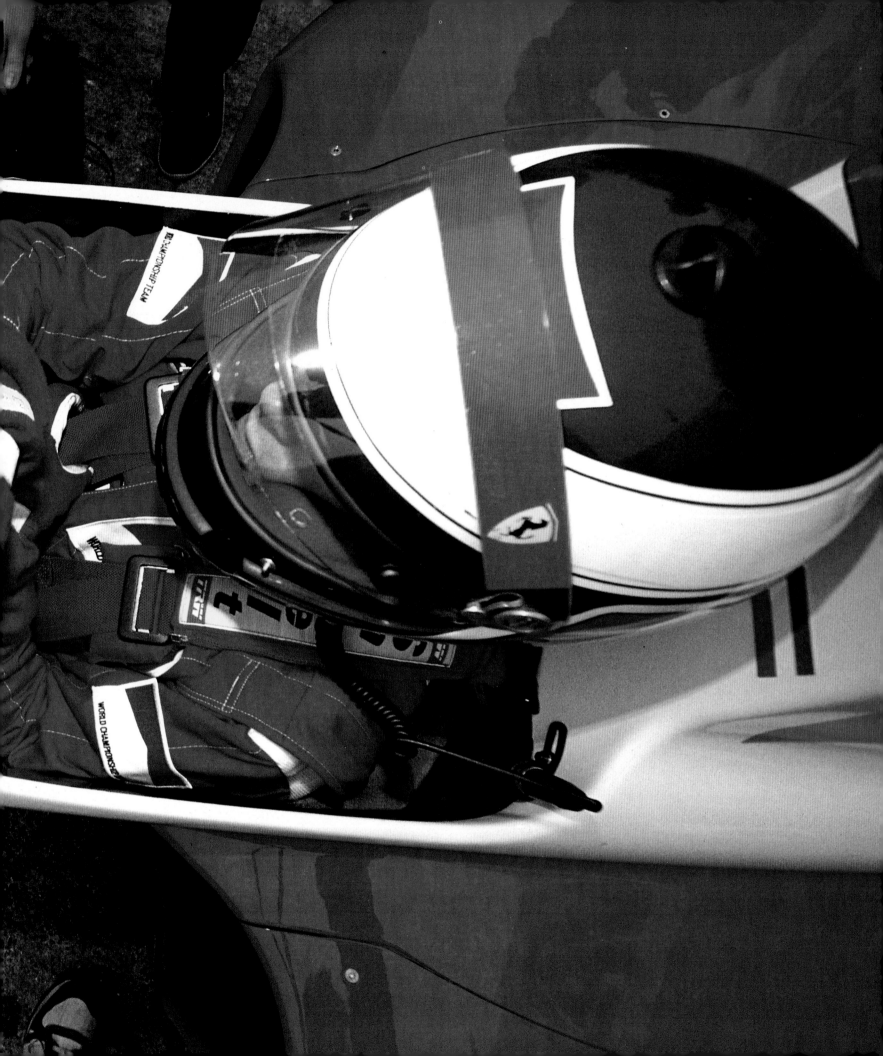

108 *Fifty men make up the team which faces the Grand Prix races of a Formula 1 season. The Ferrari team is one of the biggest and traditionally one of the most efficient.*

November 14, 1994.
Australian Grand Prix,
Adelaide. Gerhard
Berger celebrates with
Nigel Mansell after
winning second place
behind the English
driver. Mansell drove for
Ferrari in the 1989 and
1990 seasons.

Following pages.
May 28, 1995.
Monaco Grand Prix,
Monte Carlo.
The spectacular
accident at the start
of the race involving
Berger's Ferrari, Alesi's
Ferrari and Coulthard's
Williams. The start
was repeated,
and Berger won a
brilliant third place.

109

In 1996 with the arrival of Schumacher (left) and Shell, technical partner linked with Ferrari in the past, the work of renewal carried out by the team that Montezemolo wanted and Todt created can now be said to be complete.

*Opposite page.
Jean Todt was called
in 1993 to reorganize
Ferrari's racing
activities, which divide
into a number of areas.
In addition to Formula 1
are the commitments
of the Challenge
championship and
the IMSA category.
The results were not
long in coming and
in 1994 Ferrari
already had a win.
Under Todt's
management Ferrari
gained ten victories
(up to 1997).*

*Right. Michael
Schumacher showers
Jean Todt on the
podium after the 1996
Belgian Grand Prix.*

Already in his first season at Ferrari, Michael Schumacher (this page) showed all his worth by winning three races (Spain, Belgium and Italy). Things have been more difficult for Eddie Irvine, and he has been penalized also by many situations where bad luck plays a decisive role (opposite page).

Following pages. April 28, 1996. European Grand Prix, Nürburgring. Michael Schumacher during the race where he wins second place.

*September 8, 1996.
Italian Grand Prix,
Monza. Eight years
after the last victory
on the home track,
Schumacher brings
victory to Ferrari
in front of an
enthusiastic public.*

*Following pages.
September 7, 1997.
Italian Grand Prix,
Monza. Michael
Schumacher with
his Ferrari F310 B.
It was a year of further
growth. At the end
of the season there
would be five victories
(Monaco, Canada,
France, Belgium, Japan)
and the second place in
the Championship.*

122 *May 11, 1997. Monaco Grand Prix, Monte Carlo. For Irvine 1997 is the year of the come-back, in fact he won a place on the rostrum many times. Irvine raced one of his best races in Monaco, where he came third, sealing the triumph achieved by Schumacher.*

29th June 1997.
French Grand Prix,
Magny Cours. Michael
Schumacher frustrating
predictions for an
unsuccessful Ferrari
on the French circuit,
wins one of the most
decisive victories of
the Championship.

From 1996 Shell became Ferrari's most important technical partner again, resuscitating a working relationship which began way back in the fifties. There has been plenty of room for satisfaction, with 8 victories in two years.

Photo Credits

Automobilia Archives, Ferrarissima Archives, Angelo Bianchetti/Ferrari World,
Griffith Borgeson, Carrstudio, Ferrari Records Centre,
Ercole Colombo, Louis Klemantaski (The Klemantaski Collection), Gabriela Noris,
Photo 4, Maria Luisa Vaghi, Peter Vann.